Writing Effective Sales Letters

To Supercharge Your Marketing

from the library of the New Thrive Learning Institute

Get Related Materials

from Our Free Library

Instant Access – Join Here

Click or type into your browser:

http://livesensical.com/go/byob/

LEGAL NOTICE

Table of Contents

Introduction

Let's face it, if you can't write a sales letter, you can't sell your products. It's a fact. That's why we're here to walk you through our proven template piece by piece, step by step so that you can emulate it to your hearts content.

Where do you start in a sales letter? How do you create an attractive headline? How do you connect to your viewers in such a way that they can't take their eyes of your site until they're purchased your product?

We're about to answer all those questions and more. The great thing about this is you don't need to go on any extensive copywriting courses, you don't need to spend years practicing, and there's absolutely no need for you to be an expert or experienced writer in any way. As long as you can write in English, this template works every time.

Overview of Sales Letters – Part 1

- To introduce writing to sell in an easy to follow and repeatable format.

- To show you simple but effective ways of coming up with headlines that suck people into the rest of your sales letter.

- To imaginatively expand on the headline, and further pull attention through a powerful sub headline.

- To keep things interesting as we go along, still with the sole intention of selling your product, the power to captivate your readers with simple effects is easier than it seems.

- To show you what to do in each case if you get stuck for ideas or inspiration, and how to keep those ideas and your writing flowing.

- To demonstrate how quickly you can create a sales letter over the course of a few hours for long copy.

- To explain how to let your thoughts and words flow with the intention of getting the bare bones down and going back later to make it sound mouthwateringly good to your readers.

- To enforce your authority on the matter, and to offer proof for demonstration and trust building purposes without having to show bank statements with millions of dollars flowing into your account.

- To differentiate between features and solid benefits when writing your sales letters, and the importance this plays in enticing customers.

Writing Effective Sales Letters - Part 1

Welcome to the sales letter writing section. Something that can be pretty scary if you've never done it before considering the weight of it's importance. Get this wrong and no one's going to buy your stuff, which simply means no money for you. That's exactly the reason we've decided to put together a kind of step-by-step, top to bottom, start to finish explanation, allowing you to adapt on your own terms with changing times and circumstances.

Now as you've probably noticed, no matter where you go on the net, no matter what you're buying, there are all sorts of different types of sales copy and techniques around. What we're going to be concentrating on here is focused, long copy. I say long, the length varies from product to product, but it's important that you know focused single product sales letters are the most effective for marketers like us, for the simple reason it allows you to focus your marketing efforts on small but highly targeted market, send them directly to your site, and know they'll be interested.

This type of focus and organization allows us to carry out smaller targeted campaigns, and differs from the multi product sites, like online superstores in that they have a shed load more to spend on advertising than even the most efficient and profitable of us, not to mention a lot of the products us marketers come out with are generally a little more off the wall, and original with new twists and delivery methods.

Ok, so here's what we'll do. If you've ever been writing a sales letter and got stuck, or worried about your response rates, or your methods, or even never written a sales letter before, we're going to give you a quick and easy top to bottom formula to follow, and add on some rules to finish off. You don't have to be the best writer in the world, have the greatest imagination in the world, or have a masters degree anything like that. If you can write and read English, you can write effective and profitable sales letters, so lets get started.

The Attention-Grabber

First up comes the headline. The oh-so-well-known and the most apparent block of larger-than-life bold text at the head of the sales letter. So what's the intention of the headline? Well, the answer to that is twofold. Its first job is to capture the attention of the visitor. To snap them out of whatever they're doing, and divert all their attention to your copy. The second, and most importantly, it's to persuade the reader to read on. It's a short, sharp taste of what you're offering designed to make the visitor drop everything, snap out of their daily grind like trance, and listen to you.

When writing your headlines, it's important to spend a little time playing with some words. What you have to remember is that to catch this attention in the first place, your headline needs to be short, and to the point. It's not a summary of your product, and it's not just there to grab attention being completely unrelated to your product. As with your product itself you can categorize a positive headline in the same way. Solve a problem, avoid pain, or gain something that the reader wants. Your headline has to show this right away.

The how to headlines and discover headlines are popular again because they work. It really is a simple case of expressing the solutions your product offers, directly or indirectly. Let's say we're taking a marketing perspective. Here are a couple of direct headlines to start out. Discover how to make seven dollars for every dollar you spend online. Find out how to increase the size of your list ten fold in just a month. It's as easy as that. Whenever you're writing a headline, just remember the main aim of your product, the main problem it poses a solution to, or the main advantage it gives the customer, and tell them.

If you don't like the how to approach, you can always go indirect, and use the how I approach. Find out how I increased my sales tenfold in just three months with one simple technique. Watch as I create a sales system that earns me ten times my investment every month, without fail. There's nothing wrong with this approach at all. Personally, I prefer method one, telling someone directly what they can gain, but this kind of story telling method works too.

Give Your Headlines Meaning - Be Specific

Notice too that a lot of these headlines are very specific. Within three months, seven dollars for every dollar you put into your marketing, increase your list size five fold every month, and so on. This is great, because it gives an even clearer sense of focus on your product and sends out a message of individuality and confidence. This is especially true with online marketing where there's a heck of a lot of competition, and giving specific figures and stats like this is going to help you stand out and be unique against the hundred thousand million however many there are people who use the rather unimaginative 'Make more money online' headlines. Most importantly, it's going to keep people reading, for the simple reason you're no longer one of the crowd and visitors are going to read on to see what you offer instead of labeling you 'just another one of them'.

Don't Hide Your Intentions

This is why it's important not to hide the meaning of your headline or try to put off telling people about your product. If you're sending traffic to your site that's interested in your products in the first place, there's no need for you to hide anything. Factor in that if you're hiding your solution until further down the letter, why would someone read on if they've been sent to your site to find out about a seemingly different topic than you present them with?

So, as you can see, it's not difficult at all, no matter what your product. Use exact stats to stand out and be noticed, and tell your visitors about the problems you're solving, what they can gain by reading your reports, or how to avoid something unpleasant without hiding your intentions. Here are a couple more examples for you before we move on. Find out how I catch five or more specimen fish every single time I hit the water, no matter what the venue. Discover the technique that turned an amateur golfer into a competing professional in just three months. Learn how to use the software that saves me ten thousand dollars in legal fees every time I buy a new house.

I could go on forever, but I won't. One thing to remember is testing. Don't think just because you have a headline that isn't so bad that it always has to stay that way. I won't elaborate right now, because we have a whole section on effective testing later on in the course. Under no circumstances get too anxious about this, because it's not set in stone, and you can change it whenever you feel the need. Think like this, follow the above guidelines, and you'll be writing enticing and profitable headlines without that old 'Uh.. I don't know what to write' feeling coming over you. That's the first step sorted.

Attention Grabber Number 2

Next comes the sub-headline, a couple of lines of text under the main headline there for the simple reason of enforcement. It gives you a little space to expand on what you've just said and do something very important. And that's give the reader a reason to read on. Here's a well used example for you, and that's the 'don't go anywhere, because this could be the most important letter you'll ever read' approach.

Many people claim to have come up with that line, but whoever did it originally, congrats because it really does make a difference. It's kind of a settle in line. A take your hands off that mouse, don't click the dreaded x or get distracted with anything else kind of line. So that's your aim, to settle the visitor in and to stop them going anywhere.

Now personally, I'll be honest. The whole 'don't go anywhere because this could be the most important letter you'll ever read' doesn't excite me anymore, and doesn't often hold my attention. It's rather overused to say the least, and has a very 'talking at you' feel. I prefer a little something softer. Sit back in your fave chair, and relax while I show you why what you're abut to read will change the way you look at online marketing forever.

Of course there's other ways to do this too. How about 'Prise your fingers off your mouse, sit back, and take a well deserved time out while I show you something that I guarantee will change the way you look at affiliate marketing, forever. As harsh or as laid back as you'd like it to be, don't forget the reason it's there; as a feed in from your headline into your main letter. It's a 'Settle In Line'. If it meets that criteria, you're set.

Lead-In & Introductions

Next up, comes something that again, many people miss to their detriment; an introduction. Who are you? If I've just landed on your site, why should I be listening to you? Simple, tell us your name, and who you are for a start. Start by making that connection to the reader and making it personal.

Imagine you land on a sales letter with no introduction, no name, just a headline and sales letter. I guarantee you'll be reading through and be wondering who you're listening to, that's if you even read at all. The internet isn't a personal medium. People can't see your facial expressions or hear the tone of your voice. In fact, as far as anyone is concerned, if you don't introduce yourself, you're just a faceless nobody.

So here's the deal, you tell us who you are at the start of your sales letter, and we'll start listening to you as if you were a person. The easiest way to do this is a quick and easy header, 'From the desk of YourNameHere'. And what are you in relation to the product? Just the owner of the site? Designer of the software? Pioneer of this brand new fish catching system? Tell us who you are. If you're an authoritative figure, we're more likely to listen to you.

Here comes the fun part, and where most sales letters I see in my day to day browsing and exploring of the e-mails go wrong, the introduction. How to start? Well, I hope you're up for a writing a bit of a story here, because this is how I love to start the sales letters that I write. Now don't get me wrong or run a mile just yet, it's not quite as complicated as writing a make believe story. All we're going to do here is come up with a few short sentences about how first off you discovered a problem, and came up with the solution, and now you have the solution you're able to earn more cash, get more leads, catch more fish etc.

It doesn't need to be long, and it doesn't need to be complicated or awe inspiring. All you're doing here is describing the problem that you discovered and saying that you solved it with your product and to what extent. There's no reason to blab on for pages and pages if you don't want to, but this is your chance to show off your expertise, introduce your product, and lead nicely into the features and benefits section, stopping your sales letter from just becoming a big boring list.

So what exactly do you write? Well, I'll be honest with you, there's so many different ways people go about this. Your main aim is make things bigger and better. Make the problem bigger, make the solution better, make the gains bigger and avoidances more important. What I'm sure you'll find is once you're writing, like with most things, once you start, you'll flow more easily, and you won't have a problem. So, what I'll give you now is a place to start, a middle, and an end. The gaps in between you can fill with information that you believe is relevant to your product.

Where Do I Start?

So, starting out the introduction, here's an example for a list building product. Talk about how you were sitting around one day and spotted something, and wondered how the heck there's people out there with lists of hundreds of thousands and you and your marketer friends only had lists of three or four thousand. As we all know, lists are the lifeblood of online marketers, and with a hundred thousand ready to buy people at your disposal, you become one of the big guys with huge potential incomes.

(Note here that we talk about what the list does for the owner of it personally. A big list means nothing, a big list that gives you the ability to pull in thousands of dollars whenever you want to buy something, does mean something. People don't want a big list really, they want the advantages and gains a big list grants them, so expand on your points, and always talk about the advantages and freedoms each benefit gives the potential purchaser.)

So you set out and spent years researching this until you finally found a solution. This solution took your list from four thousand and doubled it every month for six months, and is still doubling today. You wanted to make one hundred percent sure it worked, so you went out and used your best marketer friend as guinea pig. It went so well, and the results were so easily replicated, you went out and tried it on a group of five marketers that had just started out. Here's what happened... (End example 1)

It works for anything, even products that you haven't created yourself. Here's another example.

Fishing - More Enticing Stories

So, here I was sitting by the riverbank in 2001, catching a minimal amount of carp. About half way through the day, this other angler comes along and sits opposite me, sets up his gear and within five minutes he's in. Twenty seven pound Carp. Half an hour later, before he's even finished setting up his other rods, he's in again, thirty two pound carp, and this is how the day went on, he pulled out one after the other. I could only imagine the amazing experiences he'd had. I wonder, are all his fishing expeditions like this?

(Note here again, we're playing on something a little different. In the previous example we talked about the list owners not wanting the list itself, but the advantages it brings. In that case it was money. In this case with the catching of all these fish, it's the adventures and experiences. A form of entertainment, which often is as powerful as the standard gaining something you want, avoiding a potential problem, and 'removing things that you don't want' themes of sales letters. Continuing;)

After about three hours of me catching nothing, and him pulling these fish out one after the other, I go on over and start talking as you do. What followed was probably the most enlightening conversation about fishing I'd ever had, and it totally opened my mind. I headed back to my swim, set up my gear all over again, and started pulling these huge fish out of the lake, and to this day, no matter the venue, or the season, I'm catching more fish than anybody else on the lake. You should see their faces! This one single conversation was so powerful and changed the way I look at fishing forever. You can imagine that immense proud feeling after every fishing trip. So naturally, I told some friends about it. And here's what happened... (End example 2)

(Again, in that example, we're playing on entertainment and gaining something again. Nobody really wants to catch more fish. They want the gains that come from catching more fish, in the above case, the immensely proud feeling.)

See how easy it is to write an enticing story that enforces the power of this product to provide a solution to a problem? Like I said earlier, this is just base for your work. You can see a clear start, middle, and end in both of these examples. Downright simple, all you're doing is talking about how you came up with it and what it's done for you in a big way, and how you don't know how you got by without it.

In addition to the above points, have you ever noticed how you enjoy hearing about other peoples lives? This is what keeps people gripped and reading. All you're doing is telling them a story related to your product that they can relate to also. If you're sending the right traffic to your sites, and they're interested in what you're talking about, they won't be able to tear their eyes off your words until you're done talking.

Feeling Your Sales Letters

In addition to this, you're playing on the advantages that come with it, the feelings, the happiness, the pride, the adventure and the entertainment. Nobody wants to catch more fish for the sake of catching more fish, but they want to do so to gain those feelings. This is such a important factor no matter what you're writing about. Really expand on those gains, because as in the above examples, a big list, lots of money, lots of fish catching, cheap cars, half price housing mean nothing on their own. It's the gains, the feelings and the avoidances attached to them, the advantages of carrying out such a task and succeeding that matter. If you're not selling those feelings, and those advantages and gains, your product on reading your sales letter will seem more like an empty shell with no meaning, than an exciting product that everyone wants.

If you're still stuck for ideas, and you're not sure how to go about this, check out some of the big name marketers that you know about and trust. Look at my sales letters. Look at Chris' sales letters and what they aim for when they start out. I can assure you, it all has a purpose, and is loosely based on this simple story telling formula to start out with. Remember though what you're writing for. I've seen some great introductions fall down because they lose sight of the goal. You're keeping the attention of the reader, and at the same time re-enforcing a practical use of your product and how it's improved the lives of yourself and your target market.

Cementing Yourself in Your Prospects Mind

Let' look at the end of the last two examples I gave you. So what did happen? Testimonials happened and your proof happened. This is your chance to really hit home about how good your product is, and how well it solves a problem, and there's two ways to do this. First, use testimonials, something that's easily requested and received by people happy with your product. If you've given it to people you know before releasing it, ask them to write something for you. If you've already released the product, ask your customers to write for you, and collect as you go along. Someone happy with a product will often tell other people about it, and that's to your advantage.

The second alternative is to use proof in place of testimonials here. Bank statements or screenshots from your payment processor to prove income from sites, photo's to prove how many fish you caught, your before-and-after scorecard from your golf rounds, things like that. Now I'm not saying that should replace testimonials, far from it. If you decide not to put testimonials in the midst of your sales letter, you can always put them down the side of your page. Both of these methods work, it's really up to you. I personally believe this adds to sales letter rather than detracts from it, but to each his own.

What both of these methods do is answer some questions going on in peoples minds. The biggest one of those being can they trust you. What we're doing here is eliminating the initial doubts quickly, and effectively without beating around the bush so to speak. Eliminating doubt and squashing fears becomes an integral part of writing your sales letter, because lets face it, anyone who writes a sales letter with the sole mindset of sell, sell, sell, isn't going to get very far without this all important element. We'll talk more about this later.

Meaty Goodness Next up comes the meaty goodness of your sales letter, and that's the main body of text that directly talks about individual parts of your product and how it's going to help the people that buy it. Again, something that many marketers get wrong is that they blab too much, one huge, dirty, disorganized body of text written in an entirely unattractive way that no one can be bothered to read. Or they just provide a list of features telling the reader what the product does. Nah! I think not.

So let's look at how to correctly go about informing your visitors about your product while keeping it interesting. First up I'd like to tell you now that the more organized approach of bullet points is the right way to go about things. It's fast to read, looks nice, and best of all if the reader isn't interested in a particular part of your product, but is interested in general, they'll be able to skip over that point and move onto the next, something that's made impossible if it's all one slog of text losing you customers. So point one here is actually use bullet points.

Of course it's never that simple, and neither is this. Something that I want you to remember, that should always form the basis of your sales letter and ad copywriting, is that listing the features is never enough. The reason for this is because it's boring, and it's breaking one of the rules of sale letter writing we talked about earlier; assumption. Just because it's totally obvious to you what something does, with so many different types of people on the internet from all around the world, it's possible that it may not be so obvious to them.

Remember, benefits sell, features don't. There's two ways to go about this as you're dissecting your product for all to see on your sales letter. Method one is to simply list the features as mini titles and in the same bullet, expand on them and talk about their benefits. The second method is similar and just mixes the two together instead of separating the feature and the benefit. Personally, I prefer method number one over method two, because it really allows the reader to see what you're getting at from the outset, and in turn lets them skip over it if they're not interested or are looking for something else in your product.

Features and Benefits Defined

I want to touch on this one more time before we end part one. Sometimes it's hard to define what's a feature and what's a benefit. There's nothing wrong with that, so before moving on I want to give you a couple of real quick examples of each. Let's look at the fishing example again. 'This product includes the ultimate fishing handbook'. Feature. 'Guaranteed to increase your catches five fold within a week of use.' Benefit. 'Featuring the top 500 places to fish in the country, including the exact locations of record catches'. Feature. 'Taking you by the hand and increasing your chances hundreds of times of getting you into the record books alongside the all time greats'. Benefit.

It's real important to know how this works, because a plain list of features may sell to people who already know what your product is about and what it does, but if you start to attract people that haven't bought this type of product before, you're losing sales, because the listed features mean nothing to them, until you tell them what it does to impact them in a positive way.

Ok that's all for the first section on sales letter writing, and I'll tell you, if you've followed this to a tee, If I'm interested in your product, up to this point I wouldn't have clicked off your page through any fault of your writing, and judging by the testing I've done with these methods, neither would a lot of other buyers.

There's more though, stay tuned for part two, where we'll talk further about re-enforcing your position, eliminating problems and worries that may arise in your potential buyers' minds, and give you some general rules to follow that apply to the whole of your sales letter. See you in part two.

Summary

Sales letter writing is something that can be pretty scary if you've never done it before, considering the weight of its importance. Bad sales letter means no one will buy your stuff, simple as that.

I'm going to show you that without being a master-class writer or having ever taken any special writing courses, you can pull together a sales letter with a solid response rate using a simple but effective, non complicated formula.

We're going to be concentrating now on long copy. That's a single product per site, which is totally focused and has one intention, and one intention only, to get people to buy your products.

It's important first to understand that we're focusing on single product long copy for now, because without a budget, or if you're just getting started, it's far easier and less costly as far as your advertising goes to find people specifically interested in the market you're catering for, instead of having to bring in a bunch of un-targeted people from different places, and just hope that they'll be interested in one of your products, and hope that they'll even find it amongst the others.

This type of focus and organization allows us to carry out smaller targeted campaigns, and differs from the multi product sites, like online superstores in that they have a shed-load more to spend on advertising than even the most efficient and profitable of us, not to mention a lot of the products us marketers come out with are generally a little more off the wall, and original with new twists and delivery methods.

Ok so here's what we'll do. If you've ever been writing a sales letter and got stuck, or worried about your response rates, or your methods, or even never written a sales letter before, we're going to give you a quick and easy top to bottom formula to follow, and add on some rules to finish off. You don't have to be the best writer in the world, have the greatest imagination in the world, or have a masters degree, anything like that. If you can write and read English, you can write effective and profitable sales letters, so let's get started.

Your attractive headline should be the starting point. The larger than life bold text at the top of the page used to grab the reader's attention immediately and pull them into reading further, and secondly give them a short sharp taste of what you're offering.

When writing headlines, it's important to spend a little time thinking about your wording. It needs to be punchy and to the point to pull the reader out of the trance of their daily grind.

How to headlines, and discover headlines are popular because they work. It's about expressing the solutions your product has to give the reader directly or indirectly.

Lets look at some examples of this from a marketing perspective. Discover how to make seven dollars for every dollar you spend online. Find out how to increase the size of your list ten fold in just a month.

Whenever you're creating your headline, remember the main aim of your product, the problem it produces the a solution for, the advantages it will give them, and tell them about it.

Your second option for your headline is the indirect story approach. Instead of telling them what they will gain, give them a taste of something you know how to do and can show them how to do. Find out how I increased my sales tenfold in just three months with one simple technique. Watch as I create a sales system that earns me ten times my investment every month, without fail.

Notice that both the direct and indirect examples above are very specific. Within three months, seven dollars for every dollar you spend on your marketing, increase your list size five fold every month, and so on.

This is done for a few reasons. One is to give greater focus on your product, and allows the reader to visualize and specifically imagine himself within a particular situation, spurring him to read on, to find out how to put himself in the situation that he wants to be in.

Second, it gives your product a sense of individuality, makes you stand out from the crowd, and inspires confidence. How many of those headlines have you seen that tell you something like 'Let me show you how to make money online'. Ignoring the fact that this is very cliché, try to visualize making money online. What do you come up with? Now try to visualize making seven dollars for every dollar that you spend. See the difference, and how much easier to is to imagine the specifics?

Find out how I catch five or more specimen fish every single time I hit the water, no matter what the venue. Discover the technique that turned an amateur golfer into a competing professional in just three months. Learn how to use the software that saves me ten thousand dollars in legal fees every time I buy a new house.

One thing to remember when looking at headlines is testing. Don't think because you have a headline that's doing ok that you can't change it, and test those changes, because often, small changes will make a big difference, here more than anywhere in your sales letter.

Also, keep in mind that your headline is not set in stone, and you can change it whenever you feel it's necessary. Think like this, follow the above guidelines, and you'll be writing enticing and profitable headlines without that old 'Uh... I don't know what to write' feeling coming over you. That's the first step sorted.

Next comes your sub-headline. This is simply a couple of lines under your headline that are placed to re-enforce you headline. It gives you a small amount of space to expand on your headline claims, and almost comforts the reader into sitting back, and continuing to read. It's a 'Take your hands off that mouse' line.

Now personally, I'll be honest. The whole 'don't go anywhere because this could be the most important letter you'll ever read' doesn't excite me anymore, and doesn't often hold my attention. It's rather overused to say the least, and has a very 'talking at you' feel. I prefer something a little softer. Sit back in your fave chair, and relax while I show you why what I'm about to show you will change the way you look at online marketing forever.

Of course there's other ways to do this too. How about; 'Prise your fingers off your mouse, sit back, and take a well deserved time out while I show you something that I guarantee will change the way you look at affiliate marketing, forever. As harsh or as laid back as you'd like it to be, don't forget the reason it's there; as a feed in from your headline into your main letter. It's a 'Settle In/Snap Out Of Your Trance and Pay Attention Line'. If it meets those criteria, you're set.

Next comes your introduction. Who are you and why should I listen to what you have to say? It creates the empathy and answers those questions immediately.

So tell us your name, and who you are for a start. Make it personal. Imagine you land on a sales letter with no introduction, no name, just a headline and sales letter. I guarantee you'll be reading through and be wondering who you're listening to, that's if you even read at all. The Internet isn't a personal medium. People can't see your facial expressions or hear the tone of your voice. In fact, as far as anyone is concerned, if you don't introduce yourself, you're just a faceless nobody. We need to fix that.

So, here's the deal. You tell us who you are from the start, and we'll start listening to you as if you were a real person.

The easiest way to do this is a simple From section at the start of your sales letter, 'From the desk of Your-Name-Here'. And why should we listen to you? To answer this, simply display yourself in relation to your product. Are you the designer or the pioneer of your product? Are you the successful business owner that your readers want to be? In these two short simple sentences, you become an authoritative figure, and the readers are immediately more likely to listen to what you have to say, and more importantly, filter down through the letter put their money in your pocket.

Next up comes the best bit, the introduction containing a little bit of a story. Often this story talks about the problems you or your customers had before using the product you're selling, and then showing what happened after you started using the product or service. Think of it as a before and after photo in words.

There are many ways to go about this, your main aim however, is to take your headline and sub-headline and begin to flow into the introduction of your product. What better lead in than to really cement in your readers mind the problems your product solved or advantages it's giving to you over the people who don't have it. Make the problems bigger and more prevalent, and make the solutions clearer, the gains bigger, and avoidances more important.

Example: So here I was, sitting by the riverbank in 2001 catching a minimal amount of carp. About half way through the day, this other angler comes along and sits opposite me, sets up his gear and within five minutes he's in, twenty seven pound Carp. Half an hour later, before he's even finished setting up his other rods, he's in again, thirty two pound carp, and this is how the day went on, he pulled out one after the other. I could only imagine the amazing experiences he'd had. Are all his fishing expeditions like this?

(Note here again, we're playing on something a little different. In the previous example we talked about the list owners not wanting the list itself, but the advantages it brings. In that case it was money. In this case with the catching of all these fish, it's the adventures and experiences, a form of entertainment, which often is as powerful as the standard gaining something you want, avoiding a potential problem, and removing things that you don't want themes of sales letters.)

I go on over and start talking as you do. What followed was probably the most enlightening conversation about fishing I'd ever had, and it totally opened my mind. I headed back to my swim, set up my gear all over again, and started pulling these huge fish out of the lake, and to this day, no matter the venue, or the season, I'm catching more fish than anybody else on the lake. You should see their faces! This one single conversation was so powerful and changed the way I look at fishing forever, so naturally, I told some friends about it. And here's what happened...

(Again, in that example, we're playing on entertainment and gaining something again. Nobody wants to catch more fish really. They want the gains that come from catching more fish, in the above case, the immensely proud feeling.)

If you're stuck for ideas on exactly what to write after the examples given above, head on over to some of the big marketers sites. Anyone you look up to, anyone you see as a success and somewhere that you want to be, and you'll see that a large majority of them use this method of storytelling to great effect.

By this point, it's likely that your powerful headline, and sub-headline pulled the reader into the letter, the introduction of yourself and your position made things more personal, created some empathy between you and the reader and through your position showed that if the reader wants what you have, they should listen to you as an authority on the subject.

Your story, or introduction makes it real. Specifics are the key here. I caught more fish using this product won't do it. Give the reader something to grab on to, something that shows them that what you're telling them is indeed a reality, and that they'll be able to achieve what you have, and if the subject matter interests them, and they want what you have, then that's a good reason for them to read on.

This method is also effective, because it keeps things interesting, personable and the reader will start to imagine and picture themselves in your position in the story from an early stage, which in turn makes them feel great and start to believe that this is possible and in turn, now they know and believe this is possible continue reading to find out how it's possible.

Now we need to take things a step further, and introduce several other parties and even more proof that what you have works. This is before we've even introduced the product itself. So what did happen to the people you taught or to the people whose product you gave?

This is your chance to really knock home how good your product is, make it even more real for your reader, spark their imagination further, and add to the trust factor, proving once and for all, what you have wasn't a one off, and it's entirely possible that the same positive things could happen to them.

Testimonials come to mind of course. A couple of short stories or thank you messages from real people to prove your worth and that your product wasn't a one hit wonder. These are relatively easy to get. Just give your friends or family your product, ask them to test it, and display the results, or even request some from your current customers. We'll talk more about this later.

Second, you have the choice of using more proof from your personal experiences, such as photo's, before and after, bank statements proving earnings is a pretty hot one nowadays.

Both of these methods go towards answering a big question in the customers mind. Can I trust this person and what they're saying? Once you've shown enough proof, and have created enough empathy with the reader, and you're over this hurdle, it's time to introduce your product.

The meaty part of your sales letter, and the main body if you will, your product. The text that talks directly about the individual aspects of your product and how it's going to assist the people that buy it.

The best way to do this is through bullet points, quick easy points that don't blab, nicely break up the page, and stop it from looking like a bundle of long tedious text.

Something that I want you to remember, that should always form the basis of your sales letter and ad copywriting, is that listing the features is never enough. The reason for this is because it's boring, and it's breaking one of the rules of sale letter writing we talked about earlier; assumption. Just because it's totally obvious to you what something does, with so many different types of people on the Internet from all around the world, it's possible that it may not be so obvious to them. Remember, benefits sell, features don't.

Make sure that each bullet point explaining a feature of your product has a benefit attached to it. There's two ways to do this. Method one is simply to list your features, and explain the benefits underneath. Method two is to mix your features in with your benefits.

Personally, I prefer method number one over method two, because it really allows the reader to see what you're getting at from the outset, and in turn lets them skip over it if they're not interested or are looking for something else in your product.

Some examples: 'This product includes the ultimate fishing handbook'. Feature. 'Guaranteed to increase your catches five fold in the first week.' Benefit. 'Featuring the top 500 places to fish in the country, including the exact locations of record catches'. Feature. 'Taking you by the hand and increasing your chances hundreds of times of getting you into the record books alongside the all time greats'. Benefit.

It's really important to know how this works, because a plain list of features may sell to people who already know what your product is about and what it does, but if you start to attract people that haven't bought this type of product before, you're losing sales simply because features mean nothing unless they benefit the buyer.

That's all for this section. What we've talked about so far will allow you to go away and begin to write your sales letters from the ground up, from the effective attention grabbing headline, to the settling in hands off that mouse sub-headline, to empathy with testimonials proof, and introductions, leading in to presenting your products benefits in an efficient, organized, clean and interesting manner, getting the most possible number of customers to actually read through what you have to say in a state of trusting and learning.

There's more, though, stay tuned for part two, where we'll talk further about re-enforcing your position, eliminating problems and worries that may arise in your potential buyers minds, and give you some general rules to follow that apply to the whole of your sales letter. See you in part two.

If you thought you had to be a master of ad copy and persuasion to sell your products, think again. As we've already shown this doesn't have to be as complex as people make out, and if you're capable of reading this report, you're capable of writing profitable sales letters again and again.

Overview of Sales Letters – Part 2

- ➤ To continue the flow of the previous section, and show you powerful additions that you can make that will increase your sales beyond what you thought your writing ability could achieve.

- ➤ To lay down some strict rules which will assist you in avoiding the pitfalls that many others fall into. Lets stop dropping your customers in the water while they're crossing that bridge.

- ➤ To re-enforce even further your personal excitement about your own products displayed through your sales letter, without tell tale hyping which will lose you sales.

- ➤ To give you a list of guarantees that you can use with your own products that are designed to push customers over the edge and hand you their cash.

- ➤ To discuss instant delivery, and how a simple few words about this can easily double your sales.

- ➤ To pay close attention to closings of sales letters, and to show you how they can be some of the most powerful tools you have in your arsenal to push more readers of the edge and turn them into customers.

- ➤ To address some general rules of sales letter writing to give your writing a real kick, and really bring it to life whilst avoiding the pitfalls of the modern day marketer.

Writing Effective Sales Letters - Part 2

In the previous section, we left off after having created an attractive headline, a settle in or sub headline, a good solid introduction, as well as concreting your expertise in the readers minds and pushing home the main benefits of your product in an effective and interesting way. Without further ado, let's continue creating your well oiled and structured sales letter.

The next step in this process is to further enhance the confidence your readers have in your product. I won't re-visit this again, as we already talked about testimonials, and proof that your product works in the previous section. Make it extra juicy, and place it right after your bullet pointed product benefits to suck the readers in a little more, starting the climb to the climax of your sales letter.

Bonuses Done Correctly

Next up comes the placement of any bonuses you may have and have decided to give away with a membership to your site or the sale of your product. When looking at what bonuses to offer, be as imaginative as you are when you create your products. It doesn't have to be an e-book or special report worth a particular amount of cash. It can be anything, even your time, maybe a free one hour consultation or something to that effect. Either way, the number one reason for adding bonuses to the end of your sales letter is simply to add value to your product. A couple of rules to remember when writing your bonuses section: First, add the price or the value, as this further gives the impression that people are getting something that's actually worth some cash, rather than a random free piece of advertising or manual that they can get for free anyway.

The second rule here is to not go over the top. Remember, even though your bonuses are related to your product in some way, you don't need to write a whole extra sales letter to sell the bonuses, because let's be honest, they're getting them either way, and you don't want to waste time or distract by going over the top with detail. A few short, quick and punchy bullets about each of your bonuses will do it. Go further, and you might find this section dilutes the initial aims of your sales letter, and that's of course to sell your product or service.

Third, and finally, don't give away too much. You're trying to push people over the edge here to buy your product, and if you give away too much and give the impression that what you're offering is too good to be true, this actually devalues the product, and shifts the focus of the bonuses being more valuable than the product itself. This leads to more doubts in your readers minds, which is not good considering that's what we're trying to squash. Keep in mind a bonus is a bonus and not your main product and you'll be fine.

Guarantees to Seal the Deal

Next come your guarantees. An integral part of any sales process is gaining the trust of your readers, and eliminating risk for them. The easiest two ways to do this are with the testimonials and proof we talked about earlier, and through guarantees.

Most importantly here, you don't want to guarantee something that you can't keep, so if you're in marketing or selling an info product, never guarantee your results no matter how confident you are in what you're doing, because some people just won't listen to what you're saying, go about things half heartedly, and then shout at you because you guaranteed them something that they didn't achieve, through no fault of your own. Aside from the moral and ethical problems with this, I believe it's also illegal and could get you and your business into trouble.

There's actually a huge amount of guarantees that you can honor in a number of different ways depending on your product or service. It's safe to say, though, that most widely used and effective are those that entail money back if something goes wrong. Standard service really, to offer a refund if things don't work out, although with intangible products this is a little more difficult. With info products for example, there's always going to be the odd time waster that tries to get your product for free and ask for a refund.

One option to avoid this is to only offer a refund on those that have taken your teachings, put them to work, and can come to you and show you that it doesn't work. Not only does this inspire a shed load of confidence in your product, again adding value and eliminating reservations in your customers' minds, but it ensures you won't get any cowboys trying to take you for a ride and get your star five hundred dollar product for free. The only catch is you have to be super confident in what you're offering at the same time.

It's definitely something that you should take some time out to ponder over if you haven't got a plan for this right away. When you're working on this, try to be specific too. A one hundred percent satisfaction guarantee doesn't hold much water nowadays if it's not tied in with something like a refund or returns policy to target a eliminate the risk, because lets face it, to take out your wallet and hand a load of cash over after reading a written page by someone you don't know takes a mighty large amount of trust.

Instant Gratification

Ok so here we are, piling on the reasons for the reader to buy your product, and squashing theirs fears and reservations at an ever increasing rate. The next thing you want to do is assure them instant delivery of something. Even if your product is due to be mailed out the next day, give them something that they can access right away.

The reason for this is just because instant gratitude is a big part of the fast paced world of the Internet. It's fast, quick and easy, allowing for impulse buys at the click of a few buttons. People want stuff quickly, and to not waste time. It's not a big thing, just remember to tell them that their copy of the product is waiting for them on the next page, or within two minutes they'll have the knowledge to beat their fishing buddies ten times over, every trip they make, small, but mighty important instant gratification.

Closing the Sale

Next up, we have something that's as important as any part of the sales process, and that is closing the sale, asking for the cash. All too often, both in the real world, and online, if you've ever trained a sales team or been on sales team that's being trained, the number one thing that'll be drilled into your head is closing the sale and asking for the cash. It's something that people just starting out don't like to do, or do in an indirect roundabout way trying to avoid this, and the fact is, the sales process can only do so much. If you don't request a signup or ask the customer to buy, it's all been for nothing.

Something else you should remember to do here is offer alternatives to the standard pricing. Just remember to try and give a little something extra to capture those people who can't afford your five hundred dollars straight up, or want to take a year's subscription at a discounted rate for your membership site giving you a big wad of cash up front.

A great way to limit the damage done by asking for the cash is to make it seem less damage than it actually is, or compare the price to something people can relate to in every day use, or enhance the gains of the product compared to it's cost. The norm seems to be comparing to a cup of coffee for a day, or lunch sandwiches for a week or something similar to that. So ask for the cash, and diminish its importance a little by relating to inexpensive every day objects.

When you're doing this though, don't make the fatal mistake of telling the reader that your super sales system only costs as much as a cup of coffee at lunch every day for a week, but remember to compare it to the advantages the customer will enjoy with your product. It's highly unlikely that your readers and potential customers are going to give you their cash if what they're getting in return isn't at the front of their minds. It's just another way of adding value and giving the readers the impression that your three hundred dollar price tag isn't actually as much as it sounds when compared to the benefits they're receiving.

Something else you may be tempted to try is hiding your price, and actually only listing it after clicking the order now link. Something that in effect will stop the reader from scrolling right down before you've sold them on all the benefits of your product and deciding it costs too much. Now, personally I don't like this one because as far as I'm concerned, if someone is really that interested to see how much this is going to set them back before they're done reading the sales letter, the sales letter isn't catchy enough and isn't doing it's job.

In my experience, this really doesn't make a big difference, if at all, so if you're following this section and writing your sales letter from it, leave it out for now, but bear in mind it's something you're free to track and test for yourself at a later date if you want to see the results for yourself.

PS

Next up, comes the PS's. I don't agree with the claims that they're the most read part of the sales letter, but I do agree that they work. They are there for one reason only, and that's to re-enforce the benefits and guarantees of your product, designed in such a way that they put the most powerful benefit, and the most powerful doubt crusher together, packaged nicely with a second order link in an attempt to push those few extra readers over the edge, and persuade them to click on your order link.

Easy as that. Follow the above guide, take into account the rules, and track everything. That's it, you're done. If you thought writing effective sales letters was hard, time consuming or you simply weren't able to do it properly, I hope to have proved you wrong with that last section..

You now know how to write attractive and catchy headlines and re-enforce correctly with sub-headlines, or the settle in line as I like to call it. Write a quick and easy connection making introduction, that's both interesting and informative for your readers, leading into the main chunk of your sales letter, defining your product and selling it's benefits. Adding value and crushing doubts in your readers minds being the final steps to that all important order link, plus a little something extra in the form of PS's to convert some extra sales.

See, it's not hard, or complicated in any way. I understand how writers block hits people sometimes, and it happens to the best of us, when we sit and stare at the screen with a blank look, not knowing how to start or continue. That'll still happen alright, but now you won't be one of the ones out there that don't know what works and how to go about it.

You won't write something now and wonder if it's totally wrong, or if anyone is going to read it, or wonder for hours on end how to structure each section. We're not done yet though, now you have the format and structure of the sales letter, there's a couple of rule sets that I'd like to go through with you. Things to keep in mind whilst writing your sales letters that will keep you and readers flowing, and to the point, and most important, get a wad load more of them to hand their cash over.

Rule 1 - No Distractions

Rule Number One: **Don't distract and confuse visitors.** The biggest problem that seems to pop up in people's sales letters is that they're confusing, or have the user click on a load of stuff to see other stuff. Now recently, someone I used to know back when I started out in online marketing went ahead and created this website. The product itself doesn't seem so bad, but the sales letter hurts my brain, even when I go over there just to see what he's doing with some spare time on my hands. Click here to see this, click here to see the features of that, hover your mouse over the little orange bit to see the pay plan, and so on.

It just doesn't work. I understand if you have a multiple product site. That may be some sort of membership that offers more than one service for example. If all the products and services are related, great, place them in bullets on the same page, allowing the reader to skip over if they're not interested. If the products are totally unrelated however, it might be time to take a look at how you're selling them and consider splitting them up into separate focused sales letters and sites. That's another issue entirely though.

For now, just remember to try and keep everything on the same page and don't divert the readers off to five or six different areas to see the benefits of each part of your product. It's plain confusing, and loses sales big time. This is probably the very first thing that I learned about structuring multi-product sales letters, with my very first site that offered ad tracking, autoresponders, conferences and a host of other stuff at the same time. Linking off to separate features just confused the heck out of my visitors, and my sales compared to targeted visitors went up more than three times after consolidating with bullets in a focused way all on the same page. Not a bad deal for a little extra work.

Rule 2 – No Constraints

Which brings me to rule number two: **Don't be constrained by length**. As I mentioned in the previous sales letter section, some of the best sales letters I've ever read that have just totally sucked me in using the same format as we've been talking about throughout this guide. Some have taken me over an hour to read, and turned out to be big selling products with great visitor to sales ratios.

So here's the thing. Don't fall into the checklist trap. A small list of features planted on a page is no match for the structure we talked about above. Now back when I first started, I wrote this big long sales letter, a little after the previous example of amalgamating all the features into one, and needless to say it was a tad large. I wasn't really all that confident about keeping things as they were, as the people that I was selling to were busy people. People who don't want to hang around for ages reading long reams of text. Or so I thought anyway.

So I went away and created this list type sales letter that I thought would do so much better, and ran a split run test with the very long and very short versions. A week and a half and twenty five new signups later from the long sales letter, and still staring at a blank from the shortened version, I had to actually check of everything was working correctly because the short version was performing so badly. Testing time was over.

I never went back. Thinking that short sales letters would outperform my long ones was probably the most profitable test that I've carried out with regards to sales letters. Without the testing though, based on the untested and incorrect assumptions at the time, it probably would have been the most expensive. Thankfully that thought was squished at an early stage.

Rule 3 - Four Elements of a Successful Sales Letter

Rule Number Three: **Your sales letter should only ever be doing one of four things, enforcing your expertise, enticing with benefits, crushing fears and doubts about your product, or asking for money.** When you're done writing, take a read through your sales letter and see if you can spot the points at which you may have deviated from your original objective, and wipe them out. Contrary to some very strange examples I've come across in my time online, there is no reason for any other text to exist other than to distract, confuse or get in the way.

We saw this example earlier, but it applies here too. See your sales letter as kind of a bridge. The starting point on one side is the headline, and anyone who successfully gets across the bridge to the other side has hit your order link and purchased your product. All those little niggly bits that have no place, all those distractions, and problem areas are giant dirty holes that customers that should have been yours, are falling through on the way to your order link. All you're doing is plugging those gaps by removing the un needed areas and distractions, and giving the best chance of a safe crossing, which of course means money in your pocket.

So here's the deal. Keep focused, rip out all those irrelevant parts of your sales letter. If it doesn't enforce your expertise, entice with benefits, crush fears or ask for cash, it plainly doesn't need to be there. Plug the gaps. Remove the dead wood. Stop losing customers through the holes.

Rule 4 - No Assumptions

Rule number Four: **Never assume anything about your readers.** There are so many renditions of this, and I'm guilty of doing this, too, in draft versions of texts. It's only natural if you've been around something for a long time that seems simple, obvious, or the norm to you. Remember it's not necessarily the norm for others. Depending on the market you're going after, there's going to be some degree of variation in the type of visitor you get and their previous experience on the subject.

There's so many variations of this, but let me give you a few examples. "Inverted commas" is a good one that seems to be taking sales letters by storm recently. When you're talking about something in a focused way, coming out with something contained in inverted commas may mean something to you, but could well mean something different to someone else, and is very easily misunderstood, along with sarcasm, irony and slang.

Rule 5 – Spice-Up Your Sales Letters

Rule number Five: **Spice it up a little.** Your writing style doesn't have to be hard sell all the way, but don't make it boring. Make it colorful, especially when you're talking about your products benefits. Remember your product isn't good. It's not cool, or nice. It's amazing, astounding, rock solid, laser targeted, and unbeatable. Get a little excited and replace some of your descriptive words with something a little more spicy and interesting.

It may sound like hard sell, but not so when coupled with my favorite writing style, which couldn't be easier for anyone to do, and that's just typing as you'd talk. It goes from hard sell TV ad sounding, and changes instantly to have a personal, but excited and confident feeling about it. There's nothing wrong with injecting your own personality either if you want to, in fact this actually adds to your sales letter. Just remember to avoid the pitfalls we talked about earlier whilst making your benefits sound a little more juicy and attractive.

Rule 6 - Keep It Structured

Rule Number 6: **Don't lose your structure.** We already talked about the four aims of your sales letter, but if you take a closer look at what we've just been discussing there's a particular structure about it. We started off with the headline, and the sub headline pulling the readers into the letter, then we went on with an intro and some reinforcement, proof and testimonials, then benefits of your product, guarantees, damage limitation making the price seem less significant, and then the PS's.

Similarly to the customers coming over the bridge example we used earlier here, notice how at each stage you're piling on the weight at an ever increasing rate, culminating in the climax and purchase of your product. The look of your product just gets better and better, and faster and faster and faster, picking up the pace and piling on those benefits, crushing those fears and doubts, and then taking your well deserved rewards in the form of a sale.

Never lose that, and never get it upside down. I've seen some backwards sales letters that pile it on for the first screen full, and by the time I'm half way down I'm bored out of my skull because they've run out of stuff to say, and I'm leaving to do something more interesting. It's the snowball effect of your sales letter, and it works like a charm.

Rule Number 7: Track and Test Everything

Finally, but most importantly **test and track everything**. Every single word you've just read has been tried and tested. Imagine what would have happened if I decided not to test and track. I guarantee you this report wouldn't be here today, not least because I'd have nothing to tell you, but also because I'd most likely be back selling stuff for other people, or taking a course somewhere on how to get a good job making someone else a bunch of cash.

There are all sorts of additions to sales letters that have been popping up for as long as I've been online, the "Yes! I understand that I'm getting..." pages that supersede order links, the "click here if you've decided not to order in the PS area at the end of the sales letters", and a whole bunch more innovative ways to increase sales and convert extra sales, but for now, just remember not to try anything new unless you're tracking it, because you'll go broke without knowing what's destroying your sales, and you'll go broke not knowing that the sentence you just deleted was responsible for 99% of your sales.

So there we have it, a complete guide and framework for creating successful sales letters for a large number of different products. One other thing I'd like you to remember is no matter how good your sales letter, if your traffic isn't quality, it won't sell. If your product isn't selling, your sales letter may not be to blame, and no amount of changing it will do any good.

Either way, you can be a lot more confident in your sales letters now. Even if you find your sales letters are a carbon copy of what I've written above, you don't have to wonder if you're going about this the right way or not. One thing that never ceases to amaze me is the ability all of us as marketers have to turn a black and white page of text, into something that through only the power of the words, can receive something that's near and dear to people, money from someone that doesn't know us, and that's never met us, and from a page that an hour earlier was blank. On a most basic level, that's very powerful and why you should always feel real proud when you make a sale, no matter how small.

Summary

Welcome to section two of the sales letter creation section of the course, where we'll continue to give you a tried a tested means of creating sales letters for your products from the very same template we, and many top marketers use to create theirs and shift large numbers of products without you having to do any extensive studying or be an expert copywriter.

We left off the last section having completed the introduction to your product, and displaying them to the reader in a clean and effective way.

The next step down the line is to further re-enforce the element of trust in the readers mind. Remember, you're doing something very powerful here, selling to people through words, people you've never met and probably never will meet in person. Let's inspire further confidence to combat this problem.

The first thing you need to do is, as we already discussed and won't go into again in detail, is add more testimonials, more proof. We've already instilled trust relating to yourself, prior to introducing the product, now we need to tie in and have your product associated with positive results.

Once you've done this, the next step is to add value. You've already got your product benefits listed, which is going to provide the base reason for your price, let's take this a step further now to show people they're actually getting more for their money than they first bargained for.

Bonuses, it's simple, it's straight forward, it's well used and it's been proven to work. The important parts here are two-fold. First, make sure your bonuses are imaginative and are there for a reason and actually relate to your product.

Your bonuses don't have to consist of e-books. In fact, it's even better if they don't. Come up with something special, something that no one else is giving away. How about a series of special additional reports written by you relating to, but not a part of the original product? How about a short free of charge, no strings attached one-on-one consultation?

There are two rules that you need to keep in mind when adding bonuses. As simple as it may seem, many violate these rules and end up devaluing their product totally, which is the opposite of what we want to achieve.

Rule one: be specific. Again, how much is your bonus worth? Give it a monetary value to demonstrate that the customer is actually getting something that's usually charged for and is worth real money. Simply giving away a free e-book with no indication of value doesn't cut it.

Rule number two: don't go over the top. All your bonuses should be related to your product in some way, and you don't need to write a whole extra sales letter for your bonuses. You definitely don't want to create any distractions from the main focus of your sales. A few short, punchy bullets outlining the value, the cost if they were to buy separately and some of the benefits they will gain is enough to do the job.

Third, and finally, don't give away too much. You're trying to push people over the edge to buy your main product. Giving away too much and inducing the too good to be true effect in readers minds, unfortunately like false and exaggerated claims will put people off and undo all that trust you worked so hard to build up in previous sections.

Ok, lets continue to pile on the trust by eliminating risk. Let's face it, people don't like spending money unless they have to, and a good way to get them to spend any in the first place is to remove risk from them, i.e., if anything goes wrong, or the sales letter doesn't do exactly what's claimed, their money will be safely returned.

Guarantees: a big confidence builder adding to previous sections. You're really building up the ammunition now, and the weight of the readers reasons to buy your product is getting stronger and stronger. Through each sentence so far you've piled on the reasons to buy. Guarantees are an integral part of that.

There are a massive number of guarantees out there to be had that you can offer, and it varies from product to product of course. It's safe to say, though, that the most widely used and effective are those that entail money back if your product doesn't do what's been advertised. No one should have any trouble doing this if their product is a quality piece.

Never guarantee your results, no matter how confident you are in what you're doing, because some people just won't listen to what you're saying, go about things half-heartedly, and then shout at you because you guaranteed them something that they didn't achieve through no fault of your own. Aside from the moral and ethical problems with this, I believe it's also illegal and could get you and your business into trouble.

Standard service really, to offer a refund if things don't work out, although with intangible products this is a little more difficult. With info products for example, there's always going to be the odd time waster that tries to get your product for free and ask for a refund. One option to avoid this (my favorite solution as it happens) is to only offer a refund on those that have taken you teachings, put them to work, and can come to you and show you that it doesn't work. Not only does this inspire a shed load of confidence in your product, again adding value and eliminating reservations in your customers' minds, but it ensures you won't get any cowboys trying to take you for a ride and get your star five hundred dollar product for free.

Buying something from someone you've never met, or don't know personally, takes a huge amount of trust. It's that trust that we're building at every turn here.

Next up, instant delivery. Even if you're mailing your product, you'll need to have something ready for people to pick up and download right away. Customers like instant gratification, getting something straight away. This course for example, if you think back to when you ordered, you would have probably received the warm-up and prep course. We did this on purpose so in effect, you could start your course right away instead of having to wait for the delivery, simple but effective.

Next, after inspiring so much confidence and putting forward our guarantees, we have to close the sale. Something people in real world sales and online marketing forget to do, asking for the money.

A great way to limit the damage done by asking for the cash is to make it seem less damage than it actually is, or compare the price to something people can relate to in every day use. The norm seems to be comparing to a cup coffee or lunch sandwiches for a week or something similar to that. So ask for the cash, and diminish its importance a little by relating to inexpensive every day objects.

When you're doing this though, don't make the fatal mistake of telling the reader that your super sales system only costs as much as a cup of coffee at lunch every day for a week, but remember to compare it to the advantages the customer will enjoy with your product. It's highly unlikely that your readers and potential customers are going to give you their cash if what they're getting in return isn't at the front of their minds.

Something else you may be tempted to try is hiding your price, and actually only listing it after clicking the order now link. Something that in effect will stop the reader from scrolling right down before you've sold them on all the benefits of your product and deciding it costs too much. Now, personally I don't like this one because as far as I'm concerned, if someone is really that interested to see how much this is going to set them back before they're done reading the sales letter, the sales letter isn't catchy enough and isn't doing it's job.

In my experience, this really doesn't make a big difference, if at all, so if you're following this section and writing your sales letter from it, leave it out for now, but bear in mind it's something you're free to track and test for yourself at a later date if you want to see the results for yourself.

Next up after your call to action comes your PS sections. I don't agree the claims of some that it's the most read part of the sales letter, but I do agree that it works like a charm.

They are here for one reason and one reason only, to re-enforce the benefits the customer would be receiving from clicking on that order link. These have to be your most benefit packed, trust building, justification adding sections, because it's the last chance you have to give your customers that extra little shove they need to be convinced to buy your products.

See, it's not hard, or complicated in any way. I understand how writers block hits people sometimes, and it happens to the best of us, when we sit and stare at the screen with a blank look, not knowing how to start or continue. That'll still happen alright, but now you won't be one of the ones out there that don't know what works and how to go about it.

Finally, I'd like to give you some set rules and guidelines for creating your sales letter in this way, and following the outlined processes above. Rule number one is don't distract and confuse visitors with dirty great popups, or masses of links reading 'click here to read this, click here to read that and see this and that.' Don't worry about the length of your copy, if it's well written and well bulleted, readers will be able to skip parts they don't care about, the odd bonuses they don't want or already own for example.

Rule number two. In addition to rule number one. Don't be constrained by length. The best sales letters I've ever read have always been long and structured. A short, small list of features and benefits planted on a single page don't do half as well as the long copy. I tested this previously with my very first site, and never went back, or even thought about going back to short copy after seeing the results.

Rule number three. Create empathy with your readers, and enforce your expertise while enticing with benefits, crushing doubts and finally asking for the cash. These are the only things your sales letter is there to do, nothing more, nothing less. If you can spot points in your copy that don't have a reason for being there, and deviate from your plan or these rules, remove it, because it's not needed and will only distract readers, and detract from your final sales figures and profits.

Rule number four. Never assume. Keep your sales letters simple and focused, and above all never assume that the reader knows what you're talking about. Remember, they can't hear your tone of voice, it's easy to misunderstand things when this is the case as you'll know if you've ever spoken to someone online or through a messenger. When you're talking about something in a focused way, coming out with something contained in inverted commas may mean something to you, but could well mean something different to someone else, and is very easily misunderstood, along with sarcasm, irony, and slang.

Rule number five. Don't be afraid to spice it up, and don't confuse this with hype. Hype is unfounded or untested spicing up a product, going so far as to give the idea that the benefits are bigger than they naturally are. Spicing something up, getting excited about your own products or its effects is nothing bad. I get excited about the stuff I create all the time, that doesn't mean I'm hyping it beyond all proportion.

It's amazing, astounding, rock solid, laser-targeted, and unbeatable. Get a little excited and replace some of your descriptive words with something a little more spicy and interesting. It may sound like hard sell, but when coupled with my favorite writing style it doesn't read like that at all. Something which couldn't be easier for anyone to do, and that's just typing as you'd talk. It goes from hard sell TV ad sounding, and changes instantly to have a personal, but excited and confident feeling about it. There's nothing wrong with injecting your own personality either if you want to, in fact this actually adds to your sales letter. Just remember to avoid the pitfalls we talked about earlier whilst making your benefits sound a little more juicy and attractive.

Rule Six. Never lose your structure unless it's for a tested and proven reason that you have yourself personally carried out and you can guarantee yourself that it works.

Notice the simple structure and starting point that we've given you for now, which you will surely develop in the future and through the launch of each of your products, piles on the reasons for buying at each stage, culminating in a final push, and the climax of the sale itself.

The look of your product just gets better and better, and faster and faster and faster, picking up the pace and piling on those benefits, confidently crushing those fears and doubts, and then taking your well deserved cash.

Never lose that, and never get it upside down. I've seen some backwards sales letters that pile it on for the first screen of text, and by the time I'm half way down the watered down second screen I'm bored because they've run out of stuff to say, and I'm leaving to do something more interesting. It's the snowball effect of your sales letter that constantly piles on the reasons to buy, and it works like a charm.

Rule number seven, finally, and most importantly, track and test your methods. Let's say for a moment that I didn't track and test anything, I guarantee you that this manual would never have gone up, and you wouldn't be reading the results today, not least because I would have had nothing to tell you, but also because I'd most likely have been back selling stuff for other people again.

There are all sorts of additions to sales letters that have been popping up for as long as I've been online, the "Yes! I understand that I'm getting..." pages that supercede order links, the "click here if you've decided not to order in the PS area at the end of the sales letters", and a whole bunch more innovative ways to increase sales and convert extra sales. But for now, just remember not to try anything new unless you're tracking it because you'll go broke without knowing what's destroying your sales and you'll go broke not knowing that the sentence you just deleted was responsible for 99% of your sales.

Remember, if your sales aren't as strong as you'd hoped, it's not always your sales letter that is to blame, it could quite easily be the quality of your traffic.

So there we have it. You now have the knowledge that you need to go out, and create profitable sales letters in a way that you know for sure sells real products. One thing that never ceases to amaze me is the ability all of us as marketers have to turn a black and white page of text, into something that through only the power of the words, can receive something that's near and dear to people, money from someone that doesn't know us, and that's never met us, and from a page that an hour earlier was blank, on a most basic level, that's very powerful and why you should always feel real proud when you make a sale, no matter how small.

Bonus

Get Related Materials

from Our Free Library

Instant Access – Join Here

Click or type into your browser:

http://livesensical.com/go/byob/

www.ingramcontent.com/pod-product-compliance
Lightning Source LLC
Chambersburg PA
CBHW021922170526
45157CB00005B/2153